WALK IN CONFIDENCE

BUILDING A HEALTHY SELF-ESTEEM

THOMAS SKARIA

Copyright © Thomas Skaria
All Rights Reserved.

This book has been published with all efforts taken to make the material error-free after the consent of the author. However, the author and the publisher do not assume and hereby disclaim any liability to any party for any loss, damage, or disruption caused by errors or omissions, whether such errors or omissions result from negligence, accident, or any other cause.

While every effort has been made to avoid any mistake or omission, this publication is being sold on the condition and understanding that neither the author nor the publishers or printers would be liable in any manner to any person by reason of any mistake or omission in this publication or for any action taken or omitted to be taken or advice rendered or accepted on the basis of this work. For any defect in printing or binding the publishers will be liable only to replace the defective copy by another copy of this work then available.

This book is dedicated to Dr Derek Boyd Murray.

A lifelong learner, teacher, counsellor and great listener. Both he and his wife (Lorna) were my mentors during my training in Pastoral care & counselling at the Baptist Hospital, Bengaluru. He left us on 25th May 2022

Contents

Testimonials — vii

Acknowledgements — xi

Foreword — xiii

Preface — xv

Introduction — xvii

1. Mary Ann Bevan — 1
2. Defining Self-esteem — 6
3. Self-esteem: Why Is It Important? — 9
4. Sources Of Low Self-esteem — 13
5. Signs & Symptoms Of Low Self-esteem — 21
6. Consequences Of Low Self-esteem — 26
7. Building Healthy Self-esteem; Using Cbt — 32
8. True Basis For A Strong & Secure Self-esteem — 41
9. Practical Steps To Improve Self-esteem — 53
10. Helping Others Develop Self-esteem — 58
11. Treasures In Jars Of Clay — 63

End Notes — 67

About The Author — 69

Other Titles — 71

Testimonials

In a world where libraries and bookstores are filled with 'self-help' books, one would wonder what new and more could come from another book on 'Self Esteem'. One must read it to appreciate this comprehensive narrative on self-esteem, from the genesis of its deficiency to the benefits of its full expression. Well researched and drawn from the works of domain experts like Freud and Maslow, the book charts the road less travelled – the Biblical basis of self-esteem. I believe it is a pragmatic and complete primer on an issue so common in today's world – a lack of self-esteem that requires building self-confidence. It does precisely that.

Besides, a book this size makes it likeable, manageable and eminently readable even on a short trans-country flight. I am sure you will then navigate the aero-bridge -walking in confidence.

- **Dr Sunil Chandy**, CMO, ITC Healthcare & Former Director, CMC Vellore

Growing up in an abusive home, in a low-income family, with addictions as young as 10 Yr old, I hated myself. I could never see anything special in myself. Not to mention that I could never see God's hand in my life. Oh, my self-esteem was battered to the core. But, I had to face it head-on.

Once I had an honest conversation with one of my mentors. This is what he wrote.

TESTIMONIALS

> *"I appreciate your radical honesty and candid sharing. The good news is that your raw honesty has surfaced an inner fault line, which otherwise would not have emerged. I could have told you of the dysfunctionalities and fault lines, but it would have little effect UNTIL you see it."*

This book on self-esteem is like Thomas holding a mirror and helping us see ourselves. This books will

- Surface our negative inner script(s) that cause us to FEEL our negative emotions and struggles.
- Help us Re-write new positive scripts that reaffirm our identity, security and sufficiency in Christ.

And one more thing. Our fault lines are often tied to an intrinsic need. We got to re-centre God as the true satisfier of our needs. His grace is sufficient for us. This is exactly what my dear friend Thomas Skaria has done through the pages of this book.

This little book on self-esteem is a lifesaver. Yes! It is, especially in our pilgrimage, in allowing God to redeem our lives for His purposes and glory.

This book is a compelling read. And indeed, an instructive one.

- **George Ebenezer**, Visionary | Teen Mentor | Counsellor

TESTIMONIALS

Confidence is the most beautiful thing you can possess. Your success will be only determined by your confidence and fortitude. For 20 years, I have known Thomas Skaria. He is one of my most precious and God-fearing students, and I have witnessed him grow in loving God and loving people.

As Thomas says in the book, our wholeness comes in full glory only through God's purpose and beauty in mind.

- **Onenlemla Imsong**, Chaplain Baptist Hosptial, Bengaluru

Acknowledgements

I want to express my gratitude to my dear wife, Aton, who has been a constant source of encouragement and support. You are a true delight and a great companion. To my son, Kevin and daughter Gracie for being the joy in my life. You both prayed for this book during our family prayers. Honestly, I was so moved by them.

To Dr Sunil Chandy, George Ebenezer and Alemla for your kind words of endorsement. Your willingness to go through the book and write these words has meant the world to me. To Dr B. J. Prashantham, professor of counselling psychology and Director of the counselling centre, Vellore, for writing the foreword. I have enjoyed our association and our phone conversations. You are a true inspiration to so many.

To Solomon Somar for working on the cover design. You have always been available, and please know your gifting is deeply appreciated.

Many others have played a pivotal role in this preaching, teaching and counselling journey. Their input into my life and insight has allowed me to see much of myself and make sense of the world around me. May the Lord bless you all. Last but not least, I want to thank my Lord, Jesus, for making me a worthy vessel in His hands.

Foreword

"You fail at things, not as a person" we need to teach our children to take failures in stride. God made you with a purpose and with everlasting love are just a few instances of wisdom distilled through stories, case studies, and personal examples to illustrate research in the book Walking in Confidence. I commend this book highly and congratulate my friend Thomas for bringing this out for the benefit and healing of many with holistic and balanced views on self-esteem.

I concur with him that self-esteem is foundational for holistic health. In eleven short chapters, he has clearly and concisely defined and shown signs, sources, and solutions to the pervasive issue of low self-esteem. Readers will benefit from the psycho-social and spiritual perspectives he provides. It is true that when you realise that you are a person of worth, you will be a wounded healer for others.

- **Dr B. J. Prashantham**. Consulting Psychologist, Professor and Director of Christian Counselling Centre, Vellore, India

Preface

Parts of this book were first spoken at the Baptist Hospital, Bengaluru. Since then, I have addressed this topic in many places, and to my surprise, it has resonated with the young and old alike. Recently, I was working on this book on my flight back from Kolkata, India and the lady who sat next to me interrupted to say that she could relate to the chapter I was working on. This, of course, set us on a long discussion throughout the flight.

Honestly, I have struggled with self-esteem. But it has taken much reading, learning, and dependence upon the Almighty, which has helped me in my own journey. I hope you, too, will learn much and be able to apply these principles in your own life so that you will walk confidently. Besides, you also will be someone who would help develop self-esteem in others, especially the ones in your family, your colleagues and those in your influence. God Bless!

- **Thomas Skaria**, September 2022

Introduction

We are thrust into a world of comparisons and competition from the time we are born. We are judged based on the colour of our skin (fair, dark, moderate brown, dark brown and so on), the size and shape of our nose (snub nose, fleshy nose, hawk nose or bumpy nose) and eyes (almond eyes, protruding eyes, monolid eyes) and various other body parameters. As we grow older, our value as a person is not only assessed by our parents but also by those around us in the community. As a child, we must excel by procuring a stunning report card and amaze others with our wisdom. We must aspire to be a head girl or a head boy at school, be good at one of the sports, or at least play a musical instrument.

Besides, attractiveness and intelligence play a significant role in finding a place for ourselves in society. This is simply evident by the constant bombardment of beauty products that offer us overnight results and beauty contests that value a certain kind of look and shape better than the others. I was intrigued to find in a school textbook the size and shape of the body that is the most preferred. It read - 36", 24", 36" figure of females is considered the best. The 'V' shape body in the case of males is regarded as the best. When a child is taught such things at the formative stages of life, they tend to believe that all those who fall below or above this specified parameter - do not fit in a normal society.

Besides, our competitive world allows only a few to be superhuman beings with extraordinary capabilities procuring exceptional jobs, leaving the rest feeling useless and hopeless. All this is because of an unjust system of evaluating our human worth.

The lack of self-esteem is not just a local problem but a universal problem affecting the rich, the poor, the mighty and the weak across people groups and languages. It impacts the old and the young and also the person with faith and without faith. For instance, I have come across people in my pastoral ministry who are well-meaning, Bible-believing Christians but, deep in their hearts, feel as if they are 'nothing' or 'totally worthless'. This sense of worthlessness often hampers them from achieving their full potential.

However, the suggestion of building healthy self-esteem must be guarded against the common idea of 'Self Worship' or 'Self Praise' prevalent in our society. Healthy self-esteem is gaining a proper understanding of who we are as a person as against what society and our culture impose upon us.

Chapter 1 is a story of a person judged based on her looks instead of her character. A story that will remind us of the cruel world of unfair comparisons and unrealistic expectations. Chapter 2 defines the term 'Self- Esteem' and brings to foreground two aspects, and illustrates how unhealthy self-esteem can manifest in two extremes. Chapter 3 discusses the importance of self-esteem. Chapter 4 lists the various sources of low self-esteem. This will help the reader to reflect on their own life and identity the root cause of low self-esteem. Chapter 5 explores the various signs of low self-esteem, and Chapter 6 discusses the impact of low self-esteem. Chapter 7 examines using cognitive behavioural therapy as an effective tool to deal with low self-esteem. Chapter 8 states that healthy self-esteem is not merely a feel-good idea but one that must rest on a good foundation. Therefore, the true basis for healthy self-

INTRODUCTION

esteem must rest on Christ and the Cross alone. Chapter 9 puts forth practical steps to develop healthy self-esteem in oneself, and Chapter 10 suggests ways in which we can help develop self-esteem in others. Chapter 11 expounds on the imagery used by Apostle Paul, 'treasure in jars of clay,' and its implications in real life.

I hope this book will enable you to live your life to its full potential, anchored on a secure base for self-esteem.

The biggest disease today is not leprosy or tuberculosis but rather the feeling of being unwanted.

MOTHER TERESA

I

Mary Ann Bevan

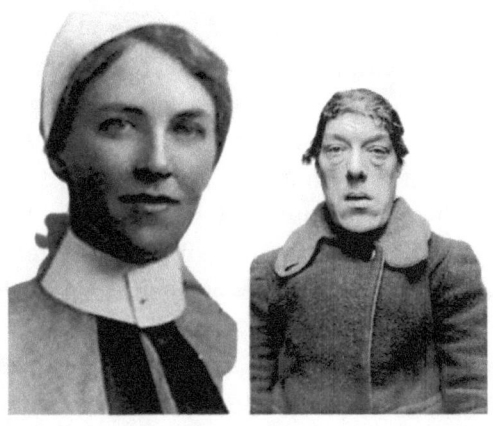

"*Mary Ann Bevan wasn't always "ugly." Born in the then-outskirts of London in the late-19th century, she looked much the same as any other young woman of the time and was even considered attractive.*"

Mary Ann Webster was born on Dec. 20, 1874, to a large family on the eastern edge of London. Throughout her childhood, she was no different from her siblings, and she eventually qualified as a nurse in 1894 before marrying Thomas Bevan, a farmer from the county of Kent, in 1903.

The Bevans settled into a happy, fruitful life, and the marriage produced two sons and two daughters, all healthy. Sadly, Thomas died suddenly in 1914, leaving Mary with four children to support on her small income. Not long after the loss of her husband, she began to show signs of acromegaly, a disorder marked by the overproduction of growth hormones in the pituitary glands.

Acromegaly is one of the rarer pituitary conditions, and today, it can be treated if detected early enough. However, under the limitations of early 20th-century medicine, Bevan had no way of treating or preventing the condition, and she soon found her features changing beyond recognition.

As a result of her condition, Bevan's otherwise normal hands and feet grew out of all proportion, her forehead and lower jaw bulged outward, and her nose grew visibly larger. Her changing looks made finding and keeping work difficult, and she resorted to odd jobs to provide for her family.

The rare condition left her permanently disfigured. Years later, a former fairground worker claimed that it was a farmer for whom she was working who told Bevan that "all [she was] fit for [was] the ugly woman competition."

Taking the farmer's words to heart, Bevan soon entered a "Homeliest Woman" contest and handily beat 250 competitors to earn the dubious title. Her victory brought her to the attention of sideshow owners, and since her doctor assured her that her condition would only grow worse, she decided to capitalise on it for the sake of her children. Soon, she had regular work in a travelling fair, appearing at fairgrounds throughout the British Isles.

In 1920, Bevan answered an advertisement in a London newspaper reading "Wanted: Ugliest woman. After mailing the agent a photo taken especially for the occasion, Bevan was invited to join the sideshow at Coney Island's Dreamland amusement park, then one of the biggest locations in the world for sideshow performers.

She was paraded alongside other sideshow acts as dreamland visitors gawked at the 154-pound she carried on her 5'7' frame. Bevan bore the humiliating treatment calmly. "Smiling mechanically, she offered picture postcards of herself for sale," all for the sake of earning sufficient money for her children's education and securing their future.

Mary Ann was perhaps one of a kind. She was resilient and used her condition to provide for her children and secure them a promising future. If only we appreciated the soul and not the looks, Mary would have been the most beautiful woman in the world.

However, the fact remains that we live in a harsh world that is constantly comparing us with each other. Not everyone is accepted or appreciated for who they genuinely are. To this day, society judges people on their physical appearance instead of their souls. Truth be told, the consuming awareness of inadequacy and inferiority is not just a local problem but a global one, perhaps an epidemic that affects people across cultures and languages.

I vividly remember the day at school; our teacher had asked us to bring the geography textbook that particular day. She entered the class and sat at her favourite place, where she could see every student through her glasses. She asked us to take our book out, and as I ran through my bag, I realised, alas, I had forgotten my geography book. Fear and trembling descended upon me as I was well aware of her temper. So, I decided to trick my teacher. I pretended to be opening my geography book, wherein I was opening another textbook. I soon fumbled towards the page she had mentioned and faked to follow every word with my finger firmly placed in the book. But my respite was short-lived. She somehow had a divine revelation; perhaps an angel of God hinted to her my trick, and I was caught. She hurled some not-so-pleasing words at me. (I shall not disclose them), which blew me apart as a student in 7th grade. Besides, she made me stand on the bench among my classmates. Can you imagine being punished in front of the girls in my class? It certainly mattered a lot to me as a boy. Whatever self-esteem I had shattered in no time.

Transactional Analysis, developed by Eric Berne (1910-1970), states that from childhood, we play the record button of an internal cassette player, which records every event, conversation, and moment into our memory. This recorder is then played and replayed in our latter years, depending on what we have learned and heard.

So, statements from my teacher and those around me get played back - forming the basis of who I am and how I perceive myself. Statements such as -

- 'You can never make it!'
- 'You are dumb!'
- 'You are an Idiot!'
- 'You will never succeed!'
- 'I wish you were never born!'
- 'You are fat!'
- 'You are black!'
- 'You are a lousy husband!'
- 'You are a boring wife!'

And so on, returns with loudness and clarity.

Dr Dobson* observes that these early feelings of inadequacy may remain relatively tranquil and subdued during the elementary school years. They lurk just below the conscious mind and are never far from awareness. But the child with the greatest self-doubts constantly "accumulates" evidence of his inferiority during these middle years. Each failure is recorded in vivid detail. Every unkind remark is inscribed in his memory. Rejection and ridicule scratch and nick his delicate ego all through the "quiet" years. Then it happens! He enters adolescence, and his world explodes from within. All of the accumulated evidence is resurrected and propelled into his conscious mind with volcanic forcefulness. He will deal with that experience for the rest of his life.*

If I ask you to transport back to your childhood, I am sure you will have many instances when people brutally assassinated your self-esteem and perhaps when your internal recorder is turned on, you still hear voices from the past, and they are loud and clear.

II

Defining Self-Esteem

Self-esteem refers to a person's overall sense of value or worth. It can be considered a sort of measure of how much a person "values, approves of, appreciates, prizes, or likes him or herself" (Adler & Stewart, 2004). However, this definition may be simplistic because of another dimension to it.

William James, the 19th Century American Psychologist, was probably the first one to venture out to understand the concept of self. He believed that each person's 'self-concept' is the view of the known self held by the knower. For example, the knower develops awareness about himself, such as being a good cricket player, good at social interactions, a tall person, etc. The self-concept develops in two ways. First, the knower watches each of these areas at work himself and, second, in interactions with other people. However, note that society's value system would validate or invalidate certain traits. For instance, a person might be a good artist, but if the culture around him values academic excellence, his being a good artist could be damning.

Both Freud (1856-1939) and Aaron Beck (1921-) acknowledge a process of 'internalising' the opinion of the significant others in forming a view of the self. According to Maslow (1908-70), esteem has two subtypes. The first is esteem reflected in others' perceptions of us, and the second is rooted in a desire for confidence, strength, independence, and the ability to achieve. So, self-esteem could be defined as -

> "*A person's overall sense of value or worth. (Internal) which is affected by the view of the significant other (culture, community, etc.). (external).*"

As you notice, two forces at work exist in how a person views themselves. No doubt, self-esteem is how we evaluate ourselves. It is our internal assessment of our qualities and attributes. But it is accessed in the context of the community and culture one is. Both these factors affect how much a person feels loved and accepted.

III

Self-Esteem: Why is it important?

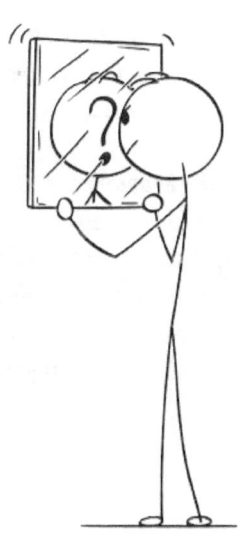

Alfred Adler (1870-1937), medical doctor, psychotherapist, and founder of the school of individual psychology, mentions that each of us is born with low self-esteem and is in constant pursuit to overcome it.

William Glasser (1925-2013), the author of reality therapy, said -

> *"All psychological problems, from the slightest neurosis to the deepest psychosis, originate due to a lack of self-esteem or a sense of personal worth."*

One way to begin to appreciate what it would be like to have higher self-esteem is to consider how we may feel about things we value in our lives - for instance, some people like bikes. Because bikes are vital to them, these people take excellent care of their bikes. They make good decisions about where to park the bike, how often to get it serviced, and how they will ride it. They may add accessories to the bike and then show it off to other people with pride. Self-esteem is like that, except it is yourself that you love, care for and feel proud of.

Abraham Harold Maslow (1908-70), an American psychologist, postulated a theory of psychological health based on fulfilling innate human needs in priority, culminating in esteem needs and self-actualisation.

According to the theory, humans possess higher- and lower-order needs, which are arranged in a hierarchy. These needs are:

- Physiological needs;
- Safety;
- Belongingness and love;
- Esteem and

- Self-actualization

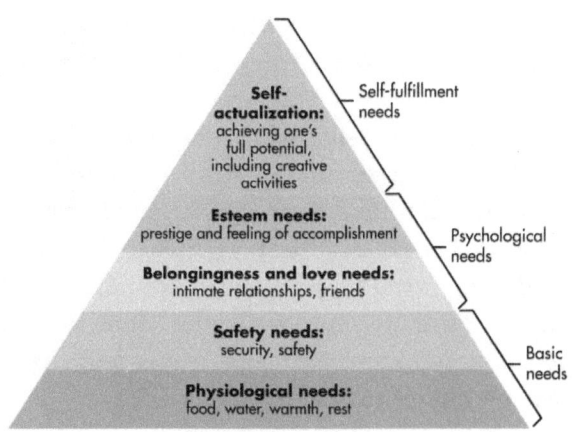

At the bottom of the hierarchy are physiological needs, considered universal. Among the physiological needs are air, water, food, sleep, health, clothes, and shelter. These needs at the bottom of the pyramid signify they are fundamental to human wellbeing and will always prioritise other needs.

Next in the hierarchy are safety needs. If a person does not feel safe in their environment, they are unlikely to guide attention toward trying to meet higher-order needs. In particular, safety needs include personal and emotional security (e.g., safety from abuse), financial security, and well-being.

Third in the hierarchy is the need for love and belonging through family connections, friendship, and intimacy. Humans are wired for connection, meaning we seek acceptance and support from others, one-on-one or in groups, such as in clubs, professional organisations, or online communities. In the absence of these connections, we fall susceptible to states of ill-being.

The fourth level of the hierarchy is esteem needs. According to Maslow, there are two subtypes of esteem.

- The first is esteem reflected in others' perceptions of us. That is the esteem in the form of prestige, status, recognition, attention, appreciation, or admiration.
- The second form of esteem is rooted in a desire for confidence, strength, independence, and the ability to achieve. Further, Maslow notes that feelings of inferiority, weakness, or helplessness will likely arise when our esteem needs are thwarted.

Dorothy Briggs asserts that self-esteem is the mainspring that slates every child for success or failure as a human being. When a child learns to accept who they are with their insufficiencies and still choose to like themselves, they grow in their emotional state. They feel more confident and secure in their interpersonal interactions.*

Adler and Horney believed that positive self-esteem was a necessary prerequisite for the ability to interact meaningfully and effectively with others. Carl Rogers worked on the assumption that if people accept themselves, they will be psychologically healthy human beings. Besides, positive self-esteem is associated with good health, satisfying relationships, tolerating and accepting others, and even hope for the future.

IV
Sources of low Self-Esteem

- **UNINVOLVED CAREGIVERS**

A hundred years ago, 99% of babies in orphanages in the United States died before they were seven months old. The babies were given modern antiseptic procedures and adequate food that should have guaranteed them at least a fighting chance for a healthy life. Nevertheless, the babies died not from infectious disease or malnutrition but a completely different kind of problem - the lack of touch. On the contrary, the condition reversed when these babies were introduced to someone who would carry them, touch them, and love them. The babies began to put on weight and grow stronger.*

When parents are busy, uninvolved or ignore their children, particularly during their growing up years, it often results in feeling forgotten, unacknowledged, and unimportant.

- **DISAPPROVING AUTHORITY FIGURES**

When one grows up hearing that they were not good enough and are criticised no matter how hard they tried, it then perpetually becomes challenging to grow into an adult with positive self-esteem.

- **PARENTAL CONFLICT**

From a very early age—as young as six months, some researchers say—children show distress when their parents fight. Their reactions can include fear, anger, anxiety, and sadness, and they are at higher risk of experiencing various health problems, disturbed sleep, and difficulty focusing and succeeding at school. Children may "externalise" their distress in the form of "aggression, hostility, delinquency, etc., or "internalise" it in the form of depression, anxiety, withdrawal and dysphoria. In addition, children from high-conflict homes are more likely to have poor interpersonal skills, problem-solving abilities and social competence.

- **ACADEMIC CHALLENGES**

When one feels they are getting further and further behind with their academics and receive no help, they might internalise the belief that they are somehow defective. They may feel preoccupied with and excessively doubt their own smartness and feel terribly self-conscious about sharing their opinions. Indeed, the feeling that one is not good enough can be difficult to shake, even after learning how to accommodate their academic difficulties.

- **INABILITY TO FIT INTO A GROUP / TRIBE**

Belonging to a 'group' or a 'tribe' is essential as it's one of our survival needs. Being different or the 'odd one out', especially during adolescence when forming one's identity, can powerfully impact their sense of self.

- **TRAUMA**

The damage that trauma exacts upon one's self-esteem also feeds into the harshness and self-hatred that frequently arises following a traumatic life event. For instance, when one is physically, sexually, or emotionally abused, it makes it hard for the person to trust the world and themselves, which profoundly impacts self-esteem. The person may disdain themselves or view themselves as repulsive and shameful, among thousand other feelings.

- **BELIEF SYSTEMS**

When one's religious or other belief system puts them in a position of feeling like they are constantly sinning or falling short of being considered worthy, it evokes shame, guilt, conflict and self-loathing.

For instance, people assume that they must become nothing, valueless - almost like criminals - putting themselves to death for God to love them truly.

- **SOAP OPERA AND SOCIAL MEDIA**

Soap Operas and TV shows are packaged carefully to showcase airbrushed models into unrealistic levels of beauty and thinness. When young people aspire to look like them, they feel miserable as they fail to measure up to what's out there, often leading to low self-esteem.

While social media is sometimes touted to combat loneliness, a significant body of research suggests it may have the opposite effect. By triggering comparison with others, it can raise doubts about self-worth, potentially leading to mental health issues such as anxiety and depression. Furthermore, social media overload may lead to problems with self-esteem, particularly in teenage girls, who are often bombarded with their friends posting perfect pictures of themselves or visiting exotic places. These can be very hard on one's self-confidence.

- **LOSS OF A ROLE**

Most of us play a host of roles in life, often moving in and out of them several times a day, such as a parent, child, student, professional, lover, friend, spouse and so on. These roles enable one to perceive themselves as playing meaningful actions in life. It adds value and significance to their existence. However, when a role is taken away - one may feel lost and misplaced—for example, the loss of a spouse, friend, parent, child etc.

Another aspect of it can be understood in terms of our roles, such as paid employment. Often who we are is defined by what we do. Thus, being a teacher, CEO, and software engineer adds to who we are as a person. However, losing such a job or a role is considered detrimental - as it may affect one's self-esteem.

- **LOSS OF HEALTH**

Loss of health due to illness can also contribute to a lack of self-esteem. I remember my time as a counsellor with The Leprosy Mission in Naini, Allahabad (Prayagraj). Part of the job was to help patients to cope with the news that they were affected by leprosy. Of course, often, the first reaction was that of denial. And the issue with denial is that if one remains in this phase, the person refuses to take the prescribed medicines, and if one does not take the medication, the disease is bound to cause more damage to their body parts. However, another obstacle that had to be crossed once patients were helped with their denial was to help with the effects of the Multi-Drug Therapy(MDT) used for treating leprosy. The face would discolour a bit due to the medicines, and girls and ladies, in particular, would stop the medication immediately as it then causes social trauma. Many of the ladies would end up in the counselling room, grieving and crying over losing self-worth due to the medicines. Of course, any illness or loss of health can trigger questions about self-image and self-worth.

- **LOSS OF IDENTITY**

Who I am and where I come from form a vital part of a person. These identities get forged at a very young age and contribute to self-esteem. Loss of land, family heritage, etc., due to war and other unforeseen circumstances may lead to loss of one's esteem. For instance, adopted children often desire to know their past for these reasons.

Besides these above sources of low esteem, Dr James Dobson observes a few other parameters that affect one's self-esteem. He says -

- **90% of our self-esteem is derived from what others think of us.**

This is corroborated by an experiment done by Solomon Asch, one of the founders of modern psychology, who carried out an interesting study.

He drew a standard line of 5 cm on the left side of the board and three other lines of 3 cm, 10cm and 5 cm, respectively, on the right side of the board. He then asked the class which lines from the three matched the size of the standard 5 cm. However, it was decided beforehand that some of Solomon's assistants would be present in the class and, when asked, would quickly answer 10 cm instead. Their collective answer, although wrong, seemed to affect the rest of the class as everyone else in the class said 10cm as the correct answer.

H. G. Wells said, "for most people, the voice of their neighbours is louder than the voice of God." "What will people say?" is one of the first questions that most of us are in the habit of asking.

Thus, whether it be a simple choice of a dress, a gadget, a motorbike, a car, a school, a college course or a more complex selection of a career, a life partner, etc. - it is all based on - what people will say.

> *"If you worry about what others will think or say, you give them influence over your future. - Jaime Villalovos"*

- Another reason for the lack of self-esteem is **we confuse failure at school and work with failure in life.**

On 9th June 2022, Hindustan Times* published the news of a class 12 student in Pune who took her life due to low marks. These are common occurrences, especially post-board exams, because one assumes failure at school as failure in life.

On 31st May 2016, the Guardian reported* that Martin Senn, 59, the former chief executive of Zurich Insurance, killed himself. Martin shot himself on 27th May, unable to live with the pain of a lost reputation. What was the lost reputation? Moral? No! Just not delivering financially what the company expected him to deliver. The failure at work was perhaps translated as failure in life - Result? Life taken!

- Lack of self-esteem is because of **an unrealistic and unfair comparison. Dr James Dobson said -**

  "*Comparison is the root of all inferiority.*"

It is observed that by comparing, one desperately attempts to preserve one's self-esteem. This process can be thought of as a compensatory form of defence. However, in the process, one feels all the more miserable.

☙

The three big lies: I am what I have. I am what I do. I am what others say about me.

HENRI NOUWEN

V
Signs & symptoms of low Self-Esteem

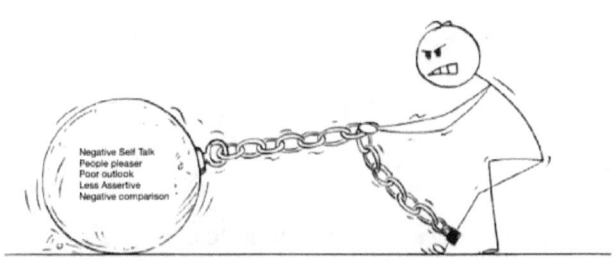

Poor self-esteem can affect emotions, thoughts, and behaviour patterns. Sometimes these signs are more obvious, but in some cases, they can be much more nuanced. Some common symptoms of low self-esteem are summarised below.

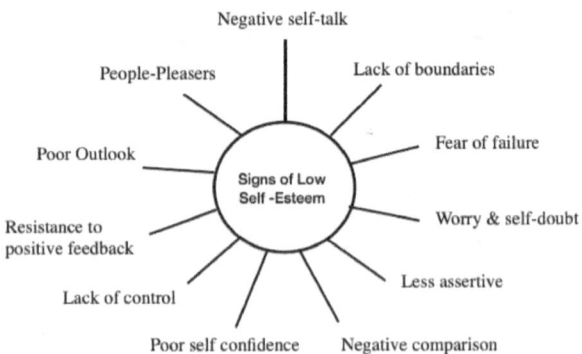

- **NEGATIVE SELF-TALK**

People with low self-esteem tend to concentrate on their shortcomings rather than their strengths. So, they tend to be pessimistic about themselves instead of building themselves with positive self-talk. They accuse themselves when things go wrong and always find a flaw with some aspect of themselves, whether it is their appearance, personality, or abilities.

- **PEOPLE PLEASERS**

While people with low self-esteem tend to talk negatively about themselves, some tend to please others to cover up for their lack of self-esteem. Either way, it affects a person's life and wellness because this often comes at the cost of neglecting one's own needs. For instance, one says yes to things they may not want to do and feels guilty about saying no.

- **LACK OF BOUNDARIES**

People with a lack of self-esteem struggle to set boundaries with other people. This is primarily because they are people-pleasers who may feel guilty or fear that people will stop liking them if they establish or maintain boundaries. The lack of boundaries adds to the stress and may make a person feel less valued.

- **POOR OUTLOOK**

It has been shown that children with negative self-esteem tend to put less effort into their endeavours because they seem to have lowered expectations of success. In adults, negative self-esteem is associated with passivity, hopelessness and compliance. These feelings can make it hard for people to engage in behaviours that will bring about positive change in their lives.

- **FEAR OF FAILURE**

Because of the lack of confidence in their abilities, people with low self-esteem distrust their ability to achieve success. As a result, they tend to either avoid challenges or give up quickly without really trying. This fear of failure can be seen in behaviours such as opting out when things go wrong or looking for ways to hide feelings of inadequacy. People might make excuses, blame external factors, or try to downplay the importance of the task.

- **RESISTANCE TO POSITIVE FEEDBACK**

Because positive feedback does not align with one's own beliefs about themselves, it is often rejected or met with suspicion and distrust. Usually, the other person is considered to be flippant or even cruel.

- **WORRY AND SELF-DOUBT**

People with low self-esteem often worry about making the wrong choice. At times, they tend to brood over their decisions, wondering if they made them right. Sometimes, they may even doubt their opinions and often defer to what others think instead of sticking to their choices. This can often lead to a great deal of second-guessing and self-doubt, which make it harder for people with low self-esteem to make decisions about their lives.

- **NON-ASSERTIVE**

A non-assertive person is one who is often taken advantage of, feels helpless, takes on everyone's problems, says yes to inappropriate demands and thoughtless requests, and allows others to choose for him or her. People with low self-esteem struggle to assert themselves and tend to get manipulated. This may further their confidence in themselves and make them feel used and abused.

- **NEGATIVE COMPARISON**

People with low self-esteem often compare themselves (in real life and on social media such as Facebook and Instagram) to people they think are better than themselves. However, comparing oneself to others can be very damaging as each person is distinct in their capabilities. As a result, one is left with feelings of inadequacy or hopelessness. Someone said -

> "*The poor image is because of comparing your worst feature to someone else's best features.*"

- **LACK OF CONTROL**

This might be because people with low self-esteem feel they have little ability to create changes either in themselves or in the world. Because they have an external locus of control, they may feel that they are powerless to do anything to fix their problems.

- **POOR SELF CONFIDENCE**

People with low self-confidence tend to have low self-esteem and vice versa. Trust in oneself means being comfortable and confident in navigating many different things in life. However, when one lacks this trust, they tend to be unable to manage life difficulties.

VI

Consequences of low Self-Esteem

The diagnostic and statistical manual of the American Psychiatric Association mentions nine types of personality disorders. Nevertheless, perhaps only two (Avoidant personality disorder and narcissistic personality disorder) out of the nine may be directly linked to low self-esteem.

- **AVOIDANT PERSONALITY DISORDER**

People with such disorders feel socially inept. They find both criticism and rejection almost impossible to cope with. They tend to view other people as superior and potentially critical of them. If people appear favourable and accepting, the avoidant personality may think, 'They don't know the real me.' These people avoid challenging social situations of any kind. They may have few relationships and would even these fewer relationships with the anxiety of potential rejection.

- **NARCISSISTIC PERSONALITY DISORDER**

It is a mental condition in which people have an inflated sense of importance, a deep need for excessive attention and admiration, troubled relationships, and a lack of empathy for others. Freud viewed a narcissistic person as stuck in an infantile world in which self-love is dominant. This is the direct opposite of the avoidant personality. But behind this mask of extreme confidence lies fragile self-esteem vulnerable to the slightest criticism. These people face problems in relationships, work, school or financial affairs. They may be generally unhappy and disappointed when they're not given the special favours or admiration they believe they deserve. They may find their relationships unfulfilling, and others may not enjoy being around them.

The Mayo clinic lays down the following signs and symptoms of this disorder.

- Have an exaggerated sense of self-importance
- Have a sense of entitlement and require constant, excessive admiration
- Expect to be recognised as superior even without achievements that warrant it
- Exaggerate achievements and talents
- Be preoccupied with fantasies about success, power, brilliance, beauty or the perfect mate.
- Believe they are superior and can only associate with equally special people.
- Monopolize conversations and belittle or look down on people they perceive as inferior
- Expect special favours and unquestioning compliance with their expectations.
- Take advantage of others to get what they want.
- Have an inability or unwillingness to recognise the needs and feelings of others
- Be envious of others and believe others envy them.
- Behave arrogantly or haughtily, coming across as arrogant, boastful and pretentious
- Insist on having the best of everything — for instance, the best car or Office

At the same time, people with narcissistic personality disorder have trouble handling anything they perceive as criticism, and they can:

- Become impatient or angry when they don't receive special treatment

- Have significant interpersonal problems and easily feel slighted
- React with rage or contempt and try to belittle the other person to make themselves appear superior
- Have difficulty regulating emotions and behaviour
- Experience major problems dealing with stress and adapting to change
- Feel depressed and moody because they fall short of perfection
- Have secret feelings of insecurity, shame, vulnerability and humiliation

- **ANXIETY DISORDERS**

Anxiety is a physical and mental state that's natural for everyone to experience at different points in time. After all, it's a state with an adaptive and protective purpose. Approximately 10% of adults may suffer this way at any time. The physical symptoms associated with anxiety are sweating, palpitations, dry mouth etc. The central theme in anxiety is believed to be a threat. The threat may be physical or psychological.

However, anxiety becomes a disorder when the intensity and duration of the emotional response are out of all proportion to the perceived threat. For example, a person may be afraid to leave the house because of appearing foolish or being rejected by people. Some may be so scared of public speaking, which is seen as a threat to one's self-esteem. Some may lie awake in bed, anxious about the possible future scenario. Again the central theme of these thoughts is often - Would I appear foolish or incompetent? Would I be accepted? These questions clearly relate to self-esteem.

Try stepping back and asking yourself questions such as

- Am I frequently blowing things out of proportion?
- Am I often distracted by thoughts of what will go wrong in certain situations?
- Do I avoid activities I might actually enjoy because of a looming feeling of dread?
- Do I constantly feel on edge or excited, even without a clear source of worry?
- Is it hurting my performance in school or at work?
- Is my anxiety hurting my relationships?

If the answers to any of these questions give you pause, or if you're finding them tough to answer, consider asking someone you trust about their perception of your anxiety and how it impacts your life.

- **DEPRESSION**

While anxiety is future-oriented emotion, depression is often associated with what has happened in the past. Beck describes three core beliefs of the depressed person in the form of a triad.

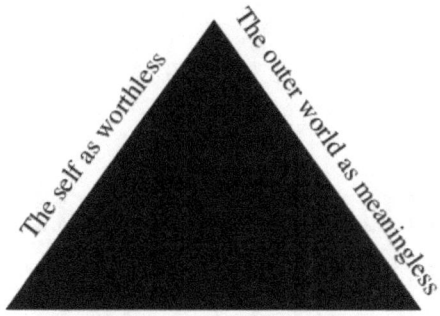
The future as hopeless

These beliefs mirror the loss of the essential aspects of the three domains involved. Thus, depressed people may feel that they deserve to be punished for numerous sins, that others would be better off without them, and that they should terminate their own existence. This hatred of self often centres around feelings of failure and rejection.

Other common problems that ensue due to low self-esteem are - eating disorders, emotional disturbance, risky behaviour, substance use and stress.

VII

Building healthy Self-Esteem; Using CBT

In my training in counselling, I was introduced to Cognitive Behavioural Therapy (CBT) associated with Albert Ellis, Aaron Beck, and Donald Meichenbaum. The cognitive-behaviour theory says that human difficulties stem from thought. It is not the event but a person's belief about it that causes emotional disturbance. The goal of this therapy is to challenge irrational thoughts and help clients separate their self-evaluation from their evaluation of their behaviour – that is, to differentiate one's identity from one's actions. I soon found this approach immensely helpful with clients. Here the therapist and the client work together to identify certain core beliefs held by the client.

The Cognitive Behavioural Model of self-esteem* (as developed by Melanie Fennell) says that -

- Throughout your life, you form negative beliefs about yourself as a result of the way you have been treated.

Psychologists call this your 'bottom line' or 'core belief'. Your core belief is how you feel about yourself deep down, for example, "I'm worthless" or "I'm no good". "To be accepted, I must be perfect'. My girlfriend didn't phone me; therefore, she doesn't love me anymore'. 'I failed at my speech; therefore, I am a failure.'

- Confronting core beliefs feels unpleasant, so we all develop rules for living that protect us from our core beliefs. These rules guide how you live your life, and your core belief stays dormant as long as your rules don't get broken. People with low self-esteem often have demanding and rigid rules, such as "I must always please other people" or "As long as I don't get criticised, then I'm OK".
- It can feel very anxiety-provoking when it seems like one of your rules might be broken. If one of your rules is "I'm OK as long as everyone is happy", it might be anxiety-provoking if people around you are not happy – you might feel that you have failed.
- When there is a danger that rules might be broken, you might make anxious predictions about what might happen and fear the worst (e.g. "I'll be rejected if I can't do everything that is expected of me"), or you might speak to yourself in a critical way, or avoid tricky situations and use strategies to cope.

Fennell states that your rules were developed to protect you but are often rather inflexible and can stop things from getting better. Although your safety strategies can make you feel good in the short term, they can keep your core belief from changing and your self-esteem from improving.

In Cognitive Therapy, the therapist challenges the core beliefs by asking the client to re-examine the evidence for their conclusions and generate alternative ways of interpreting the facts that gave rise to these thoughts in the first place.

For example - Let us assume you had a difficult upbringing, disapproving authority figures or parents who were in conflict. Perhaps you had academic challenges, or you found it difficult to fit into a group, and even worse, you were abused and traumatised. Cognitive Therapy would propose that you cannot do much with what has already happened to your life. What has happened has already happened. It is a thing of the past. But you certainly can take control of the present and deal with your 'schemas' - set belief systems and change them for a better future. Consider Cognitive Therapy as firefighters: while the fire is burning, they are not so interested in what caused it but are more focused on what is keeping it going and what they can do to put it out. This is because if they can work out what keeps a problem going, they can treat the problem by interrupting this cycle.

Let us consider a few other sources of low self-esteem that we discussed earlier and deal with the core- thought pattern. For instance, Dr James Dobson said that ***90% of our self-esteem comes from what others think of us.*** What is the core belief here? I need to please people; if I don't, they may stop liking me. And these will make me unhappy. Therefore, every decision is taken to please others, often at the cost of self-sacrifice, which may cause guilt and self-loathing. The alternative thinking is to embrace the fact that you as a person are valued and respected. You cannot live your life to please others; of course, you cannot please everyone, nor should everyone like you. So, taking responsibility for your own action despite what people might say is something you will have to work on and get comfortable with.

> "*No one on the face of the earth can make you feel inferior without your permission. - said Eleanor Roosevelt.*"

Another reason for the lack of self-esteem is the belief that ***failure in school or work equals failure in life.***

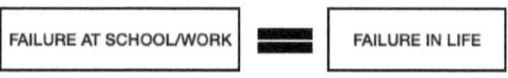

The core belief is that I must be perfect to be accepted. But if I fail at any task, I must be worthless (underlying assumption). This is an unreasonable belief because we fail at things and not as people. Failing is a stepping stone to success. Sad is it not that we are often trained to succeed and never to fail? However, I think a successful life is a life that learns from each failure and uses the lessons learned as steps to success.

- **THE DONKEY IN THE WELL**

One day a farmer's donkey fell into a well. The animal cried piteously for hours as the farmer tried to figure out what to do. Finally, he decided the animal was old, and the well needed to be covered up anyway; it just wasn't worth it to retrieve the donkey.

He invited all his neighbours to come over and help him. They all grabbed a shovel and began to shovel dirt into the well. At first, the donkey realised what was happening and cried horribly. Then, to everyone's amazement, he quieted down. A few shovel loads later, the farmer finally looked down the well.

He was astonished at what he saw. The donkey was doing something amazing with each shovel of dirt that hit his back. He would shake it off and take a step up.

As the farmer's neighbours continued shovelling dirt on the animal, he would shake it off and take a step up. Pretty soon, everyone was amazed as the donkey stepped up over the edge of the well and happily trotted off!

> "*It is not a question of IF you fail; it's a question of when - and how you respond. No successful person becomes a success without failure. - John C Maxwell.*"

The third reason for the lack of self-esteem *is **unfair and unrealistic comparisons.***

- **MAYA'S CASE STUDY**

I grew up in a family of doctors and engineers. Growing up, I always felt compared to my sister, 'the good one', 'the studious one.' Truth be told, I was more active and energetic than her, and I loved climbing trees and running around the lawn, although I often got reprimanded for the same. As I got older, people kept comparing me to my sister ("Why can't you be more like her?"), and I started to wonder if there was something wrong with me. My sister was always well-behaved at home and school. Even the school teachers compared me to her, which left me feeling like I was not good enough. I didn't achieve as well as my sister academically, so I worked for the local public school. On the other hand, my sister became a doctor, and our parents always praised her achievements. I felt like a failure and the odd one in my family.

I was burnt out at work, and my relationships were in shambles. I felt depressed as if I had failed at life. I always gave a hundred per cent, tried to do everything ideally at work, and never wanted to let anyone down, even if it meant saying yes to extra work, even when I was already overwhelmed. This meant I had little time for my partner or friends, but I worried my boss would think I wasn't up to the job if I said no. Once, I got a 3 out of 5 in my appraisal, and I felt like I was a complete failure. As a result, I worked even harder and worried about making mistakes or getting things wrong: I always put myself down.

Maya's life is a classic example of unfair and unrealistic comparison. Honestly, If you and I compare ourselves with anyone around us, we will indubitably feel inferior. Why? Because we are unique in ourselves. Each of us is rare of its kind. Out of the 7 billion plus people who have ever walked on this earth, there has been none like you. And each of us has our own distinct stories to us. So, comparison only destroys you as a person. It is contempt for your worth as a person. Getting comfortable with who you are, such as your lineage, background, pedigree, and hurts, is paramount to living a wholesome life.

For practical living, Maya, with the help of the counsellor, needs to.

- Identify her core beliefs.
- Identify her rules for living.
- Develop healthier rules and beliefs.
- Face her fears and confront the anxiety-causing situation.

- Replace self-criticism with self-compassion.
- And learn to live in line with her new core beliefs

What happens inside your head will find its way outside - into your life.

HENRY CLOUD

VIII

True basis for a strong & secure Self-Esteem

The Holy Bible points to the connection between thoughts and transformation, emphasising changing our minds so that it, in turn, may change our behaviour.

For instance, Apostle Paul reminds the church in Rome.

"Do not be conformed to the patterns of this world but be renewed by the transforming of your minds (Romans 12:2)"

"Finally, brothers, whatever is true, whatever is noble, whatever is right, whatever is pure, whatever is lovely, whatever is admirable - if anything is excellent or praiseworthy - think about such things. (Philippians 4:8)"

A significant chunk of Apostle Paul's writing is to help the new followers of Christ know who they are in Christ and how they ought to think so that they may behave correctly.

The central theme of Jesus' first message in Mathew Chapter 4 is to change. The word used there is 'Repent', meaning turn, change. Change your inner self - *your inner script* - your old ways of thinking so that you may live correctly.

This way, cognitive-behaviour theory seems more in sync with biblical principles.

However, Cognitive Behaviour therapy assumes that a person has the innate capacity to bring about an inner change. It suggests that humans are capable of self-salvation. However, the truth is - we are not! Revising our thoughts will not save us, although it may help us temporally. Dinesh D'souza* said

"We know what is right, but we lack the capacity to do what is right."

The Bible reminds us that each of us is corrupted and marred in who we are and how we think due to sin.

"All have sinned and fallen short of the glory of God - Romans 3:23"

We are given to the depraved mind to do things that are not proper, people having been filled with all unrighteousness, wickedness, greed, and evil; full of envy, murder, strife, deceit, and malice. - Romans 1:28,29

So, to have permanent and lasting self-worth, it must be attributed to us by a loving God - outside of us - who is eternal and unchanging, who, of course, changes us inside out.

- **FAITH IN CHRIST - OUR BASIS FOR TRUE SELF ESTEEM**

The Bible says, 'But God demonstrates His own love for us in this that while we were still sinners, Christ died for us'

(Romans 5:8). Our guilt, past, shame, in short, the weight of human sin was put on Jesus who bore it on the cross for us (Isaiah 53:10-12).

> "*God made Him who had no sin to be sin for us so that in Him we might become the righteousness of God - 2 Corinthians 5:21*"

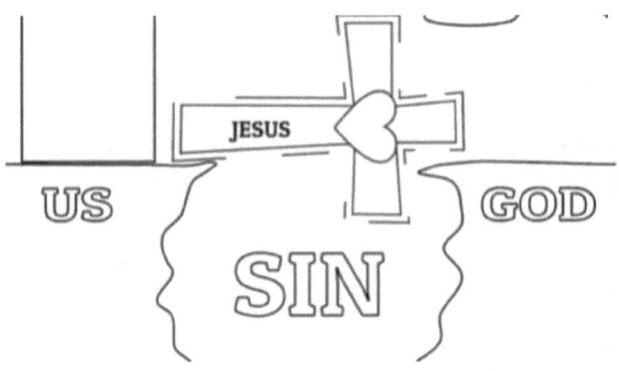

In short, *faith in Christ changes our status.* From a life inclined to sin and corruption, alienated from God, and given to irrational beliefs, we are given a new position and status as the child of God with a renewed mind and self-worth.

> "*Therefore, if anyone is in Christ, the new creation has come: The old has gone, the new is here! - 2 Corinthians 5:17*"

In Christ, we are given a new identity! Our worth now depends not on what our culture or tradition may say or what others may say - but solely on what God says to us. For instance, Apostle Paul lists the changes in our status in Ephesians Chapter 1. He says -

- **We are blessed with every spiritual blessing**(Vs 3) - People may hold their blessings from us, but in Christ, we are already blessed with every spiritual blessing.
- **We are chosen** (Vs 4)- We are not a random collection of atoms, a product of time, matter and chance. But we were considered, thought of and chosen by God even before the creation of the world. This also means you and I are by God chosen before we have done anything or have been anything for God.
- **We are adopted to sonship** (Vs 5) - William Barclay mentions that in Roman law, when the adoption was complete, it was complete indeed. The person who had been adopted had all the rights of a legitimate son in his new family and completely lost all rights in his old family. In the eyes of the law, he was a new person. So new was he that even all debts and obligations connected with his previous family were abolished as if they had never existed. God's unfolding plan for us not only includes salvation and personal transformation but also a warm, confident relationship with the Father.
- **We are accepted** (Vs 6) - Apostle Paul describes the status of accepted ('charito', which means "highly favoured" or "full of grace" as in Luke 1:28) and this status is granted to every believer because of God's grace.
- **We are redeemed** (Vs 7) - Redemption always implies a price being paid for the freedom that is purchased. The Greek word 'lootruo' is used, which means "to liberate on

the receipt of a ransom." Christ on the cross has indeed liberated us from a life of sin and wrong belief systems.
- **We have received an inheritance** (Vs 14) - Our inheritance is Christ, for Christian self-esteem is grounded in our relationship with Christ, established through faith on the basis of the cross.

Thus, I must work on my belief for any behavioural change to occur. I must believe that

- **IN JESUS, I AM MADE WORTHY**

Traditionally, our worth has been attributed to us by the family or the tradition we are born in. Our lineage and our heritage, and our community, and pedigree, mattered. Besides, our worth comes from the roles we play. For instance, you could be a father, a mother, a school teacher, an assistant professor, a chief executive officer, and so on. However, the catch is that to maintain your worth, you must prove to be a good mother, school teacher, husband, student, and so on. Thus, you are caught in the performance trap because you must constantly be doing so that you are seen as worthy. Failing at any of these roles can be catastrophic to one's self-esteem.

The Bible says - we don't have to do anything to receive our worth. My worth and your worth is not achieved, but it is received.

> *"But to all who did receive Him (Christ), who believed in His (Christ) name, He gave the right to become the children of God. John 1:12"*

- **IN JESUS, I AM VALUED**

The phrase 'Imago Dei' (Genesis 1:27) means man & woman are made in their moral, spiritual, and intellectual essence in the likeness of God. Thus, humans reflect God's divine nature in their ability to achieve the unique characteristics with which they have been endowed. These unique qualities make humans different from all other creatures:

- Rational understanding
- Creative liberty
- The capacity for self-actualisation
- The potential for self-transcendence

Imago Dei is precisely what makes every person unique and valuable, whether born with down syndrome autism or with a congenital facial deformity. Perhaps one is black or white, low caste or high caste, fair or dark, fat or lean - each carries the image of God upon them.

Everyone who receives Christ is renewed in the image that they originally meant to me. And thus, our self-esteem is based solely on the worth that Christ attributes to us.

- **IN JESUS, I AM RESTORED**

The Bible tells us about the story of a lady who suffered from the issue of blood for 12 years. (Luke 8:43-48). According to the law (Leviticus 15:25-27), excessive blood flow made a woman ceremonially unclean. Any furniture she touched was unclean as well. Other people would be unclean if they touched anything she had touched.

This woman was very alone. No one would have wanted to be around her. She couldn't go out in public. Her family couldn't hug her. Twelve years is a long time to be quarantined from all people! Not only was she considered unclean, but she probably felt it as well, having to deal with the logistics of trying to have clean clothes and linens for twelve years. She had tried to get well. She had gone to many doctors over the years. She spent everything she had trying to be cured. But nothing worked, and she even got worse!

At the moment of desperation - socially, economically, financially, physically and religiously broke- she heard of Jesus passing by. She decided to attempt to touch his garment, hoping to be healed. I wonder how she broke through the ranks and the crowd, but she managed somehow to get close enough to touch the fringes of Jesus' garment. Lo and behold, she was immediately healed. However, what she did not expect was for Jesus to stop to acknowledge her.

Mind you; this was a male-oriented society where the woman was merely a 'thing'. Moreover, she was unclean due to her condition, and her act of touching Jesus with her ailment would have jeopardised her very life. Nevertheless, Jesus addresses her 'Daughter' and says - your faith has healed you. Imagine what a consolation it must have been to be restored by Jesus. Yes, Christ restores us to Himself. It does not matter what our social-economic, financial, physical or religious conditions are. We are revived back in Christ.

- **IN JESUS, I AM ACCEPTED**

Leprosy was a terrible disease and is quite a thing even today! Most of us will cringe and pull back if we encounter leprosy affected. It isn't a pleasant sight! Something in us gets disturbed – perhaps it's to do with what we see – the ulcerated skin, truncated limbs, lumpy faces.

E. W. G. Masterman, in his article on leprosy in the Dictionary of Christ and the Gospel, says, "No other disease reduces a human being for so many years to so hideous a wreck."

The book of Leviticus details to us the ramifications of such a disease –

- The suffer was pronounced – unclean.
- He was banished from the fellowship of men (thrown away from his own family and his children and his wife)
- He must live outside of the city gates in the wilderness.
- He must cover his head and put a cover over his lips.
- And as he walked, he must shout – unclean, unclean – so that others would keep their distance from him as he walked away from the community.

In the middle ages, the priest in his stole and a crucifix in his hand would take leprosy affected into the church and read the burial service over him. A leper was a man who was already dead, though still alive.

In this context, the story is told of a leper who came to Jesus and Jesus reached out His hand and touched this man, and his leprosy left him. (Mathew 8:3). The Son of God - the holiest one did not hesitate to touch the ostracised, the most shunned in society. Can you imagine the state of this man's ecstatic emotions? No one had ever touched him for ages, not even his wife or children, but Jesus, the Son of God, did! Christ restores his self-esteem by offering him the gift of acceptance.

In another instance, Jesus accepts the lady caught in adultery and does not condemn her. Jesus was called the friend of sinners.

During my college days, I interned with an organisation that helped women caught in prostitution and rehabilitated them back into society. They also helped the children of these women to grow up in a safe environment away from the brothels by providing them food, shelter and a good education. However, I must admit, it was a struggle for these women to believe that anyone would accept them for who they were. However, with prayer, God's Word, and counselling, many were restored to living lives of dignity and worth. I recently met a girl who was part of the rehabilitation centre. She was a little girl then and struggled with her self-esteem. But today, she is married, has children, and lives a life of dignity because of Jesus' love and the acceptance of the community of Christ.

In Christ, your shameful life is welcomed. You can bring it to Jesus; He shall receive you just as you are!

> *"Therefore there is now no condemnation to those in Christ Jesus. Romans 8:1"*

- **IN JESUS, I AM EMPOWERED**

The Bible calls Satan the "father of lies" (John 8:44); if our minds are not firmly grounded in truth, then we are more susceptible to his deceptions. However, Christ empowers us to recognise these lies in the light of God's revealed Word and to demolish arguments and every pretension that sets itself up against the knowledge of God. We take captive every thought to make it obedient to Christ. (2 Corinthians 10:5)

When Jesus was baptised, the voice of God spoke over Him and said -

- **He is my son** - God, the father, confers Him with worth.
- **Whom I love** - God, the father confers Him with security
- **I am well pleased with Him** - God, the father, validates Him.

In Christ and through Christ - God confers upon each of us our worth, security and validation.

- **DOES BIBLE NEGATE THE USE OF CBT?**

The tools of CBT can be handy in seeking to take one's thoughts captive or to improve in other areas requiring self-control. It can also help combat irrational beliefs, so one is not duped into self-loathing or self-defeating behaviours. Many psychological tools can be effectively used to bring about change. However, to be genuinely free of false thoughts and grow and be fully healed, we need to be grounded in God's truth and sanctified by the power of the Holy Spirit.

When you lose focus on Christ, your mind tends to fix on what is wrong in your life instead of what is set right by the redeeming act on the cross.

IX

Practical steps to improve Self-Esteem

- **IDENTIFY SITUATIONS THAT AFFECT SELF-ESTEEM**

Some common factors that might affect your self-esteem are - a recent crisis at school, home or work. An academic challenge such as a demanding teacher or mentor, low grade. A challenging colleague or a boss at work. Change in roles in life events, such as a job loss, a child leaving home, or a health diagnosis by the doctor.

- **TAKE NOTE OF YOUR THOUGHTS & BELIEFS**

Once you have learned which situations affect your self-esteem, notice your thoughts about them. This includes what you tell yourself (self-talk) and how you view the conditions. Your thoughts and beliefs might be positive, negative or neutral. They might be rational, based on reason or facts. Or they may be irrational, based on false ideas. Ask yourself if these beliefs are true.

- **IDENTIFY THE NEGATIVE VOICE**

Be aware that it can be hard to see flaws in your logic. Long-held thoughts and beliefs can feel factual, even if they are opinions. Consider the following examples by Mayo Clinic -

All-or-nothing thinking. This involves seeing things as either all good or all bad. For example, you may think, "If I don't succeed in this task, I'm a total failure."

Mental filtering. This means you focus and dwell on the negatives. It can distort your view of a person or situation.

For example, "I made a mistake on that report, and now everyone will realise I am not up to the job."

Converting positives into negatives. This may involve rejecting your achievements and other positive experiences by insisting that they don't count. For example, "I only did well on that test because it was so easy."

Jumping to negative conclusions. You may tend to reach a negative conclusion with little or no evidence. For example, "My friend hasn't replied to my text, so I must have done something to make her angry."

Mistaking feelings for facts. You may confuse feelings or beliefs with facts. For example, "I feel like a failure, so I must be a failure."

Negative self-talk. You undervalue yourself. You may put yourself down or joke about your faults. For example, you may say, "I don't deserve anything better."

- **ACCEPT YOURSELF**

People can be very harsh to themselves. However, learn to accept 'You' as you are. Don't try to become the idealised 'YOU'. No one is perfect. Tell yourself, "I am the best me God has made."

- **FORGIVE YOURSELF**

Everyone makes mistakes. But mistakes aren't permanent reflections on you as a person. They are moments in time. Tell yourself, "I made a mistake, but that doesn't make me a bad person." Besides, research shows that change happens when our goal is to get better, not be perfect.*

- **STAY POSITIVE**

Think about the parts of your life that work well. Remember the skills you've used to cope with challenges. Give yourself credit for making positive changes. For example, "My presentation might not have been perfect, but my colleagues asked questions and remained engaged. That means I met my goal."

- **SURROUND YOURSELF WITH POSITIVE PEOPLE**

Avoid those who gossip, compare and belittle you. Stay away from others who make you feel worse.

In his books*, John Maxwell, the leadership guru, talks about the "Elevator Principle." This principle says people are like elevators. Some bring you up, and others bring you down. When you are with people who bring you up, you are encouraged, enlightened and elevated to a higher place.

- **LEARN TO BE ASSERTIVE**

You don't have to be a people pleaser. Learn to put your foot down, and draw boundaries. Practise saying 'no' and start small.

- **STAY PHYSICALLY ACTIVE**

Research has shown time and again that exercise can significantly increase your self-esteem. There are many mechanisms by which exercise increases your evaluation of yourself. For example, exercise enhances your mood and puts your mind in a more positive state. You will feel good about your physical self. Besides, get an adequate amount of sleep and eat healthy food.

- **READ YOUR BIBLE & PRAY**

Bible is God's Word to His people. It contains God's message of love and hope. It will remind you of your worth in Christ and keep you on the right track. It will also challenge your irrational beliefs and encourage you to correct them. In prayer, God will affirm His Word and remind you that you are loved, valued, accepted and validated by Christ and the finished work on the cross.

- **GET PROFESSIONAL HELP**

Consider talking to a counsellor or a therapist. They are equipped with tools to help you. Do not hesitate to seek their help.

X

Helping others develop Self-Esteem

- **ACCEPT PEOPLE**

It is so vital for us to accept people as people. We must realise that none of us is perfect. We are marred, broken people doing life. Therefore, we must be more accommodating towards others and accept them. The best gift we could give others is to accept them as they are. J.C. Ryle said -

> "*Our Lord has many weak children in His family. Many dull pupils in His school, many lame sheep in His flock, Yet He bears with them all and casts none away. Happy is the person who has learned to do likewise with his brethren.*"

- **AFFIRM PEOPLE**

Affirm people for their positive traits. This will make them feel valued. Be generous with your words. Use phrases like - I like how you... I am thankful for... I see that you are caring.. etc.

One of the things I have picked up from Krish Dhanam, a dear friend, is the art of speaking affirming words to my children. I tell both my kids these words, and they repeat them back to me -

> "*You are mine, and I love you*
> *You are terrific, and I am proud of you.*"

I want my children to know they are loved despite their weaknesses and shortcomings. Despite their accomplishments and accolades. They are appreciated for who they are.

You may also affirm people from God's Word. They are our basis for true affirmations. We may remind ourselves and others that we are redeemed, justified and sanctified, adopted into God's kingdom and that God loves with an everlasting love.

- **ALLOW PEOPLE TO FAIL**

We, as a culture, teach our children how to succeed and never coach them on what to do when they fail. And therefore, when they fail, it is considered the most shameful thing and the consequences are fatal. When the significant other knows that they are allowed to fail is when they are most productive.

- **APPRECIATE PEOPLE IN PUBLIC**

Millions of parents love their kids but, unfortunately, never tell them. Remember, applause is an effective confidence builder. Applause is so effective that in the world-renowned Suzuki method of teaching violin, one of the first things the children are taught when they are two, three and four years old is to take a bow. The instructor knows that when the children bow, the audience invariably applauds. And applause is the best motivator to make children feel good about performing and about themselves. And of course, if you ever have to correct others, do it always in private.

- **VALUE ONE ANOTHER**

It is pretty human to value high achievers and super achievers. Our school grading systems are such that the low achievers may feel they have little or nothing to offer. However, everyone has something to offer and must be valued for who they are.

- **AVOID NEGATIVE TALK**

The experienced skier knows that when they are skiing through the trees, the secret is not to look at the trees but between the trees. And the reason is if you are looking at the trees, what you get is the tree, and chances are you will hit one of those trees. However, if you keep your eyes between the trees, you will avoid the trees and keep on the path. Likewise, when we tell others - 'Don't get run over' or 'eat that, and you will be fat.' 'You are a wreck', 'you will never make it in life', and 'You are dumb' does catastrophic emotional damage. The mind begins to focus on the negatives instead of the positives.

Remember, when we give positive input, we get positive output; when we give negative input, we get negative output.

- **TREAT EVERYONE SPECIAL**

Be it the garbage picker, car driver or security guard, treat everyone with respect, for everyone is special. See each one as another human being - made in the image of God. Yes, their roles may be different; however, they are as valued and loved by God as you are.

- **LISTEN**

People with avoidant personalities believe that if people knew what they were really like, they would reject them. However, when we learn to listen to others without being judgemental and when others see that we genuinely care for them, it truly uplifts them.

- **ENCOURAGE PROFESSIONAL HELP**

Meeting with a therapist or a counsellor can be taboo in some cultures, but it is still the best help one can avail, especially when dealing with extreme cases of low self-esteem. So, if you notice the other person struggling in this area, do offer to go with them and assist them in getting help.

XI

Treasures in jars of clay

A water bearer in India had two large pots; one hung on each end of a pole which he carried across his neck. One of the pots had a crack in it, while the other pot was perfect and always delivered a full portion of water at the end of the long walk from the stream to the master's house. The cracked pot arrived only half full.

For a full two years, this went on daily, with the bearer delivering only one and a half pots full of water in his master's house. Of course, the perfect pot was proud of its accomplishments, perfect to the end for which it was made. But the poor cracked pot was ashamed of its own imperfection and miserable that it could accomplish only half of what it had been made to do.

After two years of what it perceived to be a bitter failure, it spoke to the water bearer one day by the stream. "I am ashamed of myself and want to apologise to you." Why?" asked the bearer. "What are you ashamed of?" "I have been able, for these past two years, to deliver only half my load because this crack in my side causes water to leak out all the way back to your master's house. Because of my flaws, you have to do all of this work, and you don't get full value from your efforts," the pot said.

The water bearer felt sorry for the old cracked pot, and in his compassion, he said, "As we return to the master's house, I want you to notice the beautiful flowers along the path."

Indeed, as they went up the hill, the old cracked pot took notice of the sun warming the beautiful wildflowers on the side of the path, and this cheered it some. But at the end of the trail, it still felt bad because it had leaked out half its load, and so again, it apologised to the bearer for its failure.

The bearer said to the pot, "Did you notice that there were flowers only on your side of your path but not on the other pot's side? That's because I have always known about your flaw, and I took advantage of it. I planted flower seeds on your side of the path, and every day while we walk back from the stream, you've watered them.

For two years, I have been able to pick these beautiful flowers to decorate my master's table. Without you being just the way you are, he would not have this beauty to grace his house."

> *"But we have this treasure in jars of clay to show that the surpassing power belongs to God and not to us.– 2 Corinthians 4:7"*

The Apostle Paul wrote 1 and 2 Corinthians to the church of Corinth because they were influenced by the culture that surrounded them instead of God's Word.

A potter's jar of clay is shaped and moulded before being baked and refined in the fire until the clay is hard. In ancient times, they were often used to hold things like sacred scrolls or valuable documents for safekeeping, but only temporarily.

We are referenced as a jar of clay for a few reasons. Jars of clay are just like our earthly bodies in the sense that they are temporary holding places for treasure. This life on earth is so short compared to the eternity awaiting us in heaven (James 4:14).

Like a jar of clay, we can easily be broken. Before a jar of clay is actually baked into a jar, it is just a piece of clay, easily bent and moulded. But once complete, they are very easily broken, just like us. Physically and emotionally, this world corrupt by sin will bend us and try to break us (John

10:10).

Society tells us all kinds of lies about who we are. This world says we need to look a certain way, act a certain way, be successful in this way or be a certain type of person. But the Bible is clear in explaining who we are in Him. Paul clarifies that we are all unique by calling us jars of clay. We come in different shapes, sizes, and colours and have different uses.

So, as a child of God, you and I can take heart for

- God is an artist who made us with great purpose and beauty in mind, and God has loved us with everlasting love.
- God knows our weaknesses, accepts us just as we are, and shall use us for His glory and purpose.
- God's strength is made perfect in our weakness.
- We are called to trust not in our abilities but in Christ alone, who is our true, unchanging basis for self-esteem.

End Notes

CHAPTER 1

- https://allthatsinteresting.com/mary-ann-bevan
- James Clayton Dobson Jr. is an American author, psychologist, and founder of Focus on the Family,
- https://www.drjamesdobson.org/blogs/sources-of-self-esteem-in-children-part-1-societys-infatuation-with-beauty

CHAPTER 4

- Your child's self-esteem; Dorothy Corkille Briggs

CHAPTER 4

- The Primacy Human Touch. http://www.benbenjamin.com/pdfs/Issue2.pdf
- https://www.hindustantimes.com/cities/pune-news/class-12-student-dies-by-suicide-due-to-low-marks-in-pune-101657391191407.html
- https://www.theguardian.com/business/2016/may/30/former-zurich-insurance-ceo-martin-senn-killed-himself-says-company

CHAPTER 7

- Fennell, M. J. (1997). Low self-esteem: A cognitive perspective. Behavioural and Cognitive Psychotherapy, 25(1), 1-26.

CHAPTER 8

- Dinesh D'Souza is an Indian American, political commentator, provocateur, author, and filmmaker. D'Souza has written over a dozen books, several of them New York Times best-seller.

CHAPTER 9

- https://www.mayoclinic.org/healthy-lifestyle/adult-health/in-depth/self-esteem/art-20045374
- Dr Henry Cloud, boundaries. me
- Winning with people, John Maxwell, Chapter 5

About The Author

Rev. Thomas Skaria serves as a Speaker & Ministry Director with the Life Focus Society. He holds a degree in Theology, a Diploma in Clinical Pastoral Counselling, and a master's in Psychology & Philosophy. Before joining the organisation, he served with the Leprosy Mission Trust India as a counsellor at Naini, Allahabad (Prayagraj) and later at the Headquarters in Delhi as their National advisor for spiritual nature.

His nature of work has taken him to various settings in India and Abroad, where he has addressed students at schools, colleges and conclaves. He also sets apart his time for counselling those in need, both online and in-person.

Thomas is married to Aton, and they both love and cherish the company of their two God-given children - Kevin and Gracie.

You may follow Thomas @ **Instragram:** thomasskaria80 & **Youtube:** thomaskaria

Other Titles

Order at Amazon, Flipkart or Notion PressAvailable both in Print & Kindle

www.ingramcontent.com/pod-product-compliance
Lightning Source LLC
LaVergne TN
LVHW041712060526
838201LV00043B/700